SAFETY TOWN

Bicycles Are Fun

By Dorothy Chlad

Illustrations by Clovis Martin

CHILDRENS PRESS ®
CHICAGO

This book is dedicated to Karsten and Brittney, my two granddaughters, and their mother Lyn and their father Jim—for the happiness they have given to grandma and grandpa.

Safety Town is a comprehensive educational program that introduces safety awareness and preventive procedures to preschool children. During the twenty-hour course, children learn—through their own involvement—safety rules about fire, poison, strangers, traffic, home, train, car, bus, playground, animals, toys, etc. They participate in safety activities in the indoor classroom and practice safety lessons on the outdoor layout, which consists of a miniature town complete with houses, sidewalks, and crosswalks. Role-playing in simulated and real-life situations, under the guidance of a teacher and uniformed personnel, provides children with learning experiences. This allows them to respond properly when confronted with potentially dangerous situations that occur in everyday life.

National Safety Town Center, established in 1964, is the pioneer organization dedicated to promoting preschool-early childhood safety education. This nonprofit organization has been largely responsible for enlightening the media, corporations, government officials, and the general public to the importance of safety education for children. Its network of dedicated volunteers continually supports and promotes the importance of safety for children through the Safety Town program.

Note: Bicycles are shown without reflectors because young riders should not ride their bicycles at night.

Library of Congress Cataloging-in-Publication Data

Chlad, Dorothy.
    Bicycles are fun / by Dorothy Chlad;
illustrated by Clovis Martin.
        p.   cm. — (Safety Town)
    Summary: Two children enjoy riding their bicycle
and tricycle and always try to follow the safety
rules.
    ISBN 0-516-01971-6
    1. Cycling—Juvenile literature. 2. Cycling—
Safety measures—Juvenile literature. [1. Bicycles
and bicycling—Safety measures. 2. Safety.]
I. Martin, Clovis, ill. II. Title.
III. Series: Chlad, Dorothy, Safety Town.
GV1034.5.C45   1992   92-12193
796.6—dc20   CIP
                                         AC

For more information about the
Safety Town program
please contact
    National Safety Town Center
    P.O. Box 39312
    Cleveland, Ohio 44139
    216-831-7433

95-632 ✓

Hi, my name is
Karsten and this is my
sister Brittney.

3

This is my bicycle.
Mom and Dad gave it
to me for my birthday.

This is Brittney's tricycle.

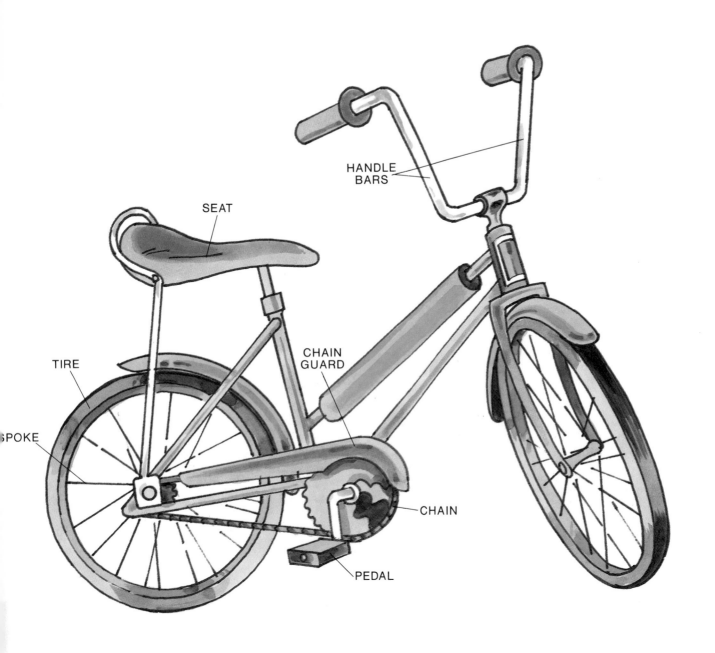

HANDLE
BARS

SEAT

CHAIN
GUARD

TIRE

SPOKE

CHAIN

PEDAL

Mom and Dad
showed me all the
parts of my bicycle.

Before I ride my bicycle, I check its parts. If any parts are loose or broken, we fix them.

Then I ALWAYS put
on my helmet.

Mom and Dad check
Brittney's tricycle and
help her put on her
helmet.

My sister and I ride in
our driveway and on
the sidewalk.

We are very careful
when we pass people
on the sidewalk.

Sometimes I ride with my Mom. Before we cross the street, we look left—right—left.

We live on a busy street. There are a lot of cars, trucks, buses, and motorcycles. I cannot ride in the street.

My friends ride in the
country. They must be
very careful, too.

Sometimes Dad takes Brittney for a ride on his bicycle. They ALWAYS wear helmets.

My family has a lot of fun. We ride to the playground, to the store, and to the library.

Sometimes we ride
to the park to watch
Mom play baseball.

On special days,
Mom helps me
decorate my bicycle.

24

Dad helps
Brittney
decorate
her tricycle.

Then we ride in the parade.

When I am done riding, I ALWAYS put my bicycle away. I put it in a safe place so it does not get broken.

Dad puts Brittney's tricycle away.

You can have a lot
of fun on your bicycle,
if you remember our
bicycle safety rules:

1. ALWAYS wear your helmet.

2. Ride where Mom and Dad tell you.

3. Check your bicycle parts.

4. Fix loose or broken parts.

5. Put your bicycle in a safe place.

6. ALWAYS be careful.

About the Author

Dorothy Chlad, founder of the total concept of Safety Town, is recognized internationally as a leader in Preschool/Early Childhood Safety Education. She has authored eight books on the program, and has conducted the only workshops dedicated to the concept. Under Mrs. Chlad's direction, the National Safety Town Center was founded to promote the program through community involvement.

She has presented the importance of safety education at local, state, and national safety and education conferences, such as National Community Education Association, National Safety Council, and the American Driver and Traffic Safety Education Association. She serves as a member of several national committees, such as the Highway Traffic Safety Division and the Educational Resources Division of National Safety Council. Chlad was an active participant at the Sixth International Conference on Safety Education.

Dorothy Chlad continues to serve as a consultant for State Departments of Safety and Education. She has also consulted for the TV program. "Sesame Street" and recently wrote this series of safety books for Childrens Press.

A participant of White House Conferences on safety, Dorothy Chlad has received numerous honors and awards including National Volunteer Activist and YMCA Career Woman of Achievement. Dorothy Chlad accepted the **President's Volunteer Action Award** from President Reagan for twenty years of Safety Town efforts. In 1986 Cedar Crest College in Pennsylvania presented her with an honorary degree, Doctor of Humane Letters. She has also been selected for inclusion in **Who's Who of American Women**, the **Personalities of America**, the **International Directory of Distinguished Leadership, Who's Who of the Midwest**, and the 8th Edition of **The World Who's Who of Women**.

About The Artist

Clovis Martin has enjoyed a varied career as an art director, designer, and illustrator of children's books and other educational products. Two books illustrated by Mr. Martin were selected for the prestigious "Children's Choices" list, a project of the IRA/Children's Book Council. He lives with his wife, two daughters, and his son in Cleveland Heights, Ohio.